THE HOMEWORK SQUAD'S
ADHD GUIDE TO SCHOOL SUCCESS

Books for Kids From the
American Psychological Association
maginationpress.org

Book design by Rachel Ross
Printed by Phoenix Color, Hagerstown, MD

Library of Congress Cataloging-in-Publication Data
Names: Shifrin, Joshua, author. | Bishop, Tracy Nishimura, illustrator.
Title: The homework squad's ADHD guide to school success/by Joshua Shifrin, PhD, ABSNP, NCSP, ADHD-CCSP; illustrated by Tracy Nishimura Bishop.
Description: Washington, DC : Magination Press, [2021] | Summary: "Bite-size tips and interactive journal entries to help kids recognize how they learn best and act on that knowledge"—Provided by publisher.
Identifiers: LCCN 2020047130 (print) | LCCN 2020047131 (ebook) | ISBN 9781433833755 (hardcover) | ISBN 9781433837173 (ebook)
Subjects: LCSH: Attention-deficit-disordered children—Education—Juvenile literature.
Classification: LCC LC4713.2 .S45 2021 (print) | LCC LC4713.2 (ebook) | DDC 371.94—dc23
LC record available at https://lccn.loc.gov/2020047130
LC ebook record available at https://lccn.loc.gov/2020047131
Manufactured in the United States of America
10 9 8 7 6 5 4 3 2 1

THE HOMEWORK SQUAD'S
ADHD GUIDE TO SCHOOL SUCCESS

By Joshua Shifrin, PhD, ABSNP, NCSP,
ADHD-CCSP

Illustrated by Tracy Nishimura Bishop

MAGINATION PRESS · WASHINGTON, DC · AMERICAN PSYCHOLOGICAL ASSOCIATION

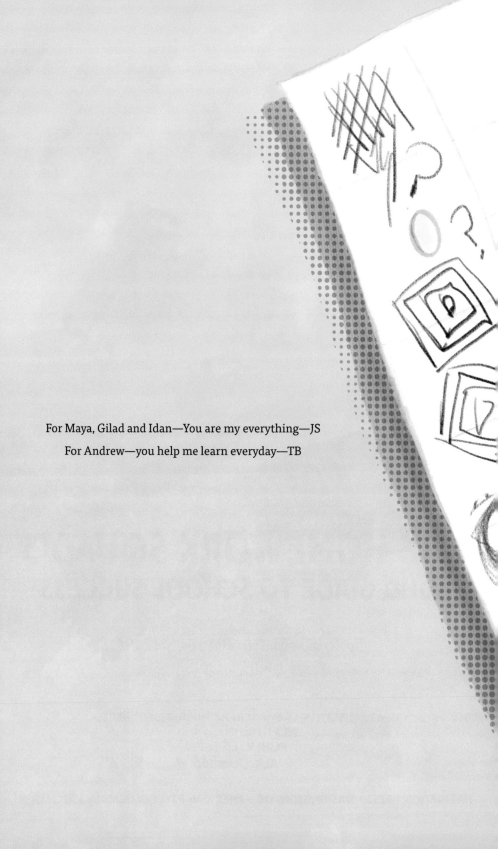

CONTENTS

A WORD FROM THE HOMEWORK SQUAD

My name is Hunter. My mom says I'm driven by a motor, whatever that means. All I know is I can't sit still. I tap my feet. I play with my pencil. I've even fallen out of my seat right in the middle of class! Can you imagine anything more embarrassing?

I try to pay attention. I swear I do. But sometimes, when I really try to listen to my teacher, I start to daydream about listening to my teacher. Crazy, right? Well, if you're reading this book, I guess you can relate.

I have what's called Attention Deficit Hyperactivity Disorder, aka ADHD. I know I'm not stupid. It's weird, but if I'm interested in something—I mean really interested—I can focus. I memorized all the hometowns and colleges of the best players on my favorite football team—go Wombats!—and I'm a good problem solver. I can fake a fever by running around my room and building up a good sweat to get out of babysitting my little sister, Jade. I'm also funny. Jade doesn't think so, but what does she know?

My parents tell me that my ADHD is part of what makes me special. I guess that's true, but it can also be totally annoying. It drives me crazy when Dad tells me to try harder to pay attention. Does he think I want to be this way?

Sometimes ADHD can be a real pain in the you-know-what. It's just so hard to sit in class and listen. And don't even get me started on homework. So, finally, I got sick of struggling and decided to do something about it. Remember, I'm a problem solver!

I got permission from my parents and Principal Wilson to put up fliers at school. Principal Wilson opened the doors for me bright and early before everyone got to school so no one would know it was me who put up the fliers. This is what they said:

If you have ADHD, struggle to stay focused, or just want to get better grades, meet in room 223 right after school. —Your ADHD buddy

To be honest, I was kind of afraid no one would come. Or everyone would come and laugh at me. So, you can imagine how psyched and terrified I was when three kids from my class showed up.

Michael is the tallest kid in the grade and an awesome athlete. He gets picked first for every team, but he's really cool about it. I mean, he could score every time if he wanted to, but he still passes the ball. Even to the kids who aren't very good. No ego, if you know what I mean.

Prisha has this head of long, curly brown hair and is super nice. She even brought in personalized cupcakes with these awesome star sprinkles for her birthday. She wrote everyone's name in strawberry frosting.

The third is Mateo, the class clown. He tells the best jokes and always cracks everybody up. Like in science, when he told us not to trust atoms because they make up everything, or in music when he asked us what Mozart was doing in his grave. (Decomposing!) He can even burp the entire alphabet.

The craziest thing is none of us knew the others had ADHD too. We got to talking about how our ADHD affects us. And not just the bad, but the good as well.

Prisha said her ADHD makes her more artsy. I've seen her stuff—the whole school has—and she's an amazing artist! She came in first in the art fair two years in a row and creates "found art" out of objects that are not supposed to be art at all.

Mateo said his ADHD makes him funnier because his mind is always thinking of new jokes, even when he's not trying! Most kids play sports after school, but Mateo does this acting thing called improv where he and a bunch of other actors get on a stage without a script and just wing it. I can see how he'd be good at that kind of thing.

Michael said his ADHD helps him think up plays on the basketball court that no one else can. He sees the chalk in his brain drawing up the Xs and Os on a mental chalkboard and everything. Coach Humboldt lets him call plays sometimes. And he has never, ever let a sixth grader call his own plays!

As for me, well...I guess I can come up with really creative stories, which helps a lot when I have to put my sister Jade to sleep. She won't go down without a bedtime story. One I whipped up, about a goblin wolf named Gabagool who turns a whole village into meatball people and eats them one by one, gave her nightmares for a week! But I thought it was funny.

Prisha, Mateo, Michael, and I agreed that our ADHD helps us do well at certain things but not as well as others.

For one thing, we all have trouble focusing in class. Michael and I have a hard time sitting still. I tap my pencil. Michael bounces his knee like a basketball, especially when he's taking tests. He's usually one of the last to finish.

Mateo sometimes blurts out the first thing that comes into his head. This gets him in trouble sometimes when he doesn't raise his hand, or when he asks a question that someone else already asked, sometimes right before him.

And no matter how hard she tries, Prisha can't seem to stay focused on a reading assignment for five minutes before she starts to daydream (about art, I suppose). It's the same as when I'll sometimes roll off into writing a story when I should be taking notes, then realize what I'm doing and look at the clock and see that ten minutes has passed. Ten minutes of notes down the drain.

The thing is, even though we were all kind of embarrassed to talk about the bad, it was really cool how we could relate to each other. And by that point, I had the courage to ask the group a question about something that always made me feel like an idiot.

I said, "Have you guys ever read something and totally forgot what you just read?"

As soon as I said it, I regretted it. But then all three of them—Prisha, Michael, and Mateo—jumped out of their seats and screamed "Yes! OMG, yes!"

It was the first time I ever truly believed other kids had the same experiences with ADHD as I do. Something about the looks in Prisha and Mateo and Michael's eyes told me they were thinking the same thing. Then a thought popped into my head: "Why don't we stick together?" It was the best thought I ever had!

We decided to call ourselves the Homework Squad. We made a pact:

1. Meet every Tuesday after school.

2. Research at least one study skill each week to help our ADHD.

3. Test the skills together.

4. Add every skill that works to our super-sacred, ultra-official guidebook:

**THE HOMEWORK SQUAD'S
ADHD GUIDE TO SCHOOL SUCCESS**

We've now met for a whole school year and have come up with over 100 amazing ADHD study skills. We even brought on our own mad scientist to help us with our experiments!

Dr. Joshua Shifrin—or as we like to call him, "Shiff"—used to teach at the college down the road. He's a neuropsychologist and has his own practice where he helps kids like us with ADHD. The cool thing about Shiff is he has ADHD symptoms, too! So, he gets it. He's the perfect expert advisor.

SHIFF

And the best part of the Homework Squad? All of us have gotten better grades and school has become less difficult and embarrassing. I mean, let's face it, it's still school. But it's much better now than it used to be.

I can sit still for longer periods of time without tapping my pen or letting my pencil run away from me with a story. We found that it helps me to visualize what Mrs. Cavoli is saying in the form of a story in my mind. Which is like the best of both worlds for me, because I get to spin a web and not miss out on the lesson.

Prisha can focus for longer than five minutes on a reading when she starts to daydream. Crazy enough, we discovered that doodling helps her stay focused. Counterintuitive, I know! But it works for her. Doodling is a non-distracting activity that soothes a restless mind.

Mateo can catch his thoughts before they come out of his mouth spontaneously. We learned about a technique called "internal monologue," where you repeat what the teacher is saying in your own words in your head. So, Mateo transformed Mrs. Cavoli's voice into an old British gentleman's voice in his mind. It's so Mateo, yet his British thoughts keep his sudden ADHD thoughts from cropping up in class. He still forgets to raise his hand, but his grades are up!

And Michael is doing much better on tests. We found that if Michael takes time to read over the entire test first, it actually saves him time in the end. He understands what's ahead of him and this puts his mind, and his bouncy knee, at ease. He can drive through the test like he drives to the hoop!

Take it from us, it feels great to be a better learner. And I have to admit, when I come home with good grades, seeing the expression on my parents' faces makes me feel even better. I know it sounds corny, but I'm proud of myself. And believe it or not, there are times when I actually like school.

We've put all of our ADHD study skills into this book. It took a lot of work, a whole year, but it's been entirely worth it! Not to mention the added bonus of finding three new best friends. We're all learning more and getting higher grades.

Mateo even says he wants to be a teacher if the whole improv thing falls through. Prisha will probably be a world-famous artist. Michael could just as easily make it to the NBA and have his own line of sneakers.

As for me? Maybe I'll be an author, or director, or even an actor! One thing's for sure, I'll always have the best stories to tell my kids at bedtime! But for today, we're just trying to get through Picklebury Middle School.

The Homework Squad discovered that some ideas kept popping up over and over again in our research. We decided to label these skills the "Kingdom Keys," because they are so important for unlocking an ADHD brain. Some Kingdom Keys include:

- **PACE, DON'T RACE.** Many ADHD students want to finish every assignment quickly before they get bored, or because it's overdue. Slowing down can actually help them finish faster.

- **BREAK IT DOWN.** ADHD students can feel overwhelmed by thick books, big projects, or long tests. Breaking an assignment into small pieces can be the key that unlocks success.

- **SET GOALS AND REWARD YOURSELF.** Build in rewards for your hard work. Treat yourself when you reach a goal.

- **PRACTICE.** Any skill worth truly mastering is going to take practice. We know it's a cliché, but practice really does make perfect.

These key skills turn up in some form in most of the chapters because they are fundamental to developing good study habits.

In each chapter, the Homework Squad listed the most common challenges we faced. For each challenge, we've put together the tricks that worked for us. At the end of each chapter, you'll find a fun journal prompt that encourages you to try out one of the tricks and reflect on whether or not it worked for you. We don't expect every single trick to be a good fit for you (that would be slightly weird), which is why it's a good idea to try them on for size. We suggest grabbing a separate journal. Go ahead and answer some or all of the questions once you read the chapter and decide which tricks you'd like to use in the future.

We hope our study skills guide can help you like it's helping us—maybe you could even form a homework squad in your own school. You never know what you can accomplish until you try, and the support of friends can make all the difference.

Your friend in ADHD,
—Hunter, Co-Chair of the Homework Squad

P.S.—We even gave ourselves Homework Squad nicknames: Pencil Tap Hunt, Prishi Daydreams, Matty Blurttles, and Mikey KneeBounce. Guess who's who! It's important to own your quirks, you know? It's what makes you, you!

JOURNAL PROMPTS

1. Who does this book belong to?

2. What is your superpower?

3. What is your Homework Squad nickname?

4. Why are you reading this book?

Have you ever read something and then had no idea what you just read? Us, too! Teachers ask us to do more reading than anything else. And of course, reading is one of the most difficult skills for kids with ADHD. No wonder so many of us end up hating reading or thinking we're terrible readers (wrong!). If you struggle with reading, know you're not alone.

The five main reading challenges for kids like us are comprehension, focus, long assignments, boredom, and silence. But don't worry! The Homework Squad has collected tricks related to each of these challenges that will help you read more easily, understand your reading better, and enjoy reading more.

CHALLENGE: COMPREHENSION

Of all the reading challenges we listed, comprehension should be at the top of the list. It can be *so frustrating* to read and read and have no idea what the material is about. The following skills can help you understand even the most difficult reading assignments.

TRICK: MAKE A MAP

For many students with ADHD, opening your textbook is kinda like going to the dentist. You don't know what's coming, but you can bet your allowance it will be painful...but it doesn't have to be. The cool thing about a textbook, though (the only cool thing), is that you can see what's coming if you take the time to look. Shiff says it's important to keep the big picture in mind and not get lost in the details. So before you begin, look over the material. Ask yourself, "What might the title mean?" Peek at all the section headings. Then read the introduction and conclusion very carefully. Finally, read the chapter summary. When you survey before you read, you create a roadmap for what lies ahead. When you start reading, the text is much easier to understand. Taking a little extra time at the beginning will save you a lot of time in the end!

 Michael

This trick works great for me because I can visualize the material, just like a basketball play on the court. Suddenly, it makes sense to me!

TRICK: TAKE A PEEK

If you're reading a chapter book (not a textbook), there's still a way to survey the material before you read. You'll think we're crazy when we tell you this, but it's a-okay to look at an online summary. This is not cheating, it's understanding. Enter a few magic words into a search engine and voila! By reading an online summary first, you'll understand the actual book better when you read it. If you know what's going on, you can actually enjoy the story!

TRICK: RELATE NEW TO OLD

Reading can be extra difficult when it's about a new topic. See if you can relate the new subject to one you've already learned. For example, if you're reading about Alexander the Great, try to relate him to someone you've read about before, or someone you know or saw on TV. Maybe Alexander the Great's conquests remind you of your favorite athlete or musician, or Iron Man! By relating old information to something more current, you'll be much more likely to remember it for the long run.

TRICK: DOODLE

Not a note-taker? No worries. Doodling is a fun alternative to jotting down notes. For some of us, words just aren't enough. Pictures stick with us. Draw an illustration that represents the material in visual form. Artistic students find that doodles make it easier to comprehend what they've read. And as Shiff told us, sometimes the more outrageous/silly/crazy the doodle, the more you'll remember it come test time.

TRICK: USE YOUR OWN WORDS

A final trick to comprehend your reading is to put it into your own words. So many ADHD students try to comprehend their reading material by repeating the information exactly as it's written. And if you've ever tried this technique, we don't have to tell you it's likely to end in wasted time and a whole bunch of frustration. But by putting your reading material into your own words, you can turn that defeat into a win. For example, if you're reading about "highly combustible elements" you can rephrase it as "stuff that can explode." We can better understand things and remember information by saying them our way. So at the end of a paragraph or page or chapter, take a break to translate.

CHALLENGE: FOCUS

The second reading barrier that is sure to give you trouble is difficulty focusing! If there's one main issue most ADHD students struggle with, it's their ability to pay attention. And this inattention monster is likely to rear its ugly head while reading. But you're in luck, because the Homework Squad has come up with skills that can improve your ability to focus and make that seemingly impossible reading passage a more pleasurable experience.

TRICK: BOOKMARK IT

Ever lose track of where you are when you're reading? Do your eyes jump from one part of the page to another and lose their place? Shiff says if he had a nickel for every ADHD student who tells him they lose their place while reading...well, let's just say he'd be a very rich man. But not to fear, the Homework Squad has a simple solution to this common problem. Take a bookmark, or just a piece of paper, and place it under the line of text you're reading. When you finish reading the underlined material, slide your bookmark down to the next line. This simple technique helps you keep your eyes on the prize.

TRICK: HIGHLIGHT AND UNDERLINE

Grab your trusty highlighter or favorite pen and highlight or underline the important information as you read. This easy technique keeps you focused on the text.

Prisha

I love this trick. It keeps my attention on the words instead of some faraway place.

Make sure not to highlight or underline everything, because then you can't tell what's actually important. A trick for pinpointing what's most relevant is finding the bolded or italicized text and the words that follow—these are likely key definitions you will need to know later! You can also look for keywords such as "in conclusion" or "most important" and focus on the information associated with them. When you're done, or when you study, open the book back up and reread the highlighted material in your notebook for a quick refresher.

TRICK: RE-READ

Because one of the main difficulties for most ADHD students is a lack of focus, it only makes sense that when you're reading a passage in a textbook your mind may, at times, be elsewhere. Sound familiar? It might be tempting to just keep on going. Don't! Take the time to re-read the material. We know this can be frustrating. But repetition breads comprehension, as we like to say in the Homework Squad. Re-reading may take you more time, but your grades will thank you for it in the end.

TRICK: BE AN EARLY BIRD

Don't put off your daily reading until too late at night. We know it can be tempting to put a dreaded assignment off as long as possible. But trust the Homework Squad when we tell you this will only come back to bite you in the end. You'll feel behind, and your day will be full of stress with the assignment hanging over your head like your own personal storm cloud. Knock out some pages in the morning, Early Bird. Get a good night's sleep, wake up early, and karate chop the reading in half. It feels good to be productive before the day starts.

TRICK: READ WHAT INTERESTS YOU

Whenever your teacher lets you choose what to read, take advantage! But don't just pick the shortest possible book or article. A short length doesn't mean the reading will be easy or enjoyable. Find something that actually interests you, even if it's a little longer. It's easier to focus and comprehend when you enjoy the material.

CHALLENGE: LONG ASSIGNMENTS

We get it! You already hate reading and now your teacher gives you a super-long reading assignment. Is there anything worse?! Before you start to pull your hair out, test these tried and true Homework Squad skills to help tackle even the longest of reading tasks.

TRICK: SCRIBBLE

It's difficult to sit still long enough to read a whole chapter. If this sounds like you, and it probably does if you're anything like the members of the Homework Squad, try scribbling while reading. Scribbling is a non-distracting activity and a healthy prescription for the fidgets. It soothes the nerves and allows you to concentrate on the task at hand. So the next time you're struggling to get through pages and pages of reading material, break out the scratch paper, grab that pen or pencil, and get at it.

HUNTER

If I'm not distracted by my little sister, Jade, running around, it's the pencil that I can't stop tapping on my desk. I discovered I can actually draw boxes over and over on the page while reading and keep my focus.

 (WARNING: If you have trouble multitasking this solution is NOT for you.)

TRICK: SKIMBOARD

A long reading assignment can feel like a mountain on your chest. Especially for those of us who process information a tad bit slower, or who may have to read something two or three times to understand it. But if you are pressed for time, or are feeling overwhelmed, don't be afraid to skim some of the reading. Say you have five long reading tasks for the week: first skim all of them. Decide which ones are the most difficult and important. Read those word for word. Then, read the easier ones and/or the less important material a bit more quickly. Skimboarding helps you prioritize during crunch time.

TRICK: MAKE BITE-SIZE CHUNKS

If you're overwhelmed before diving into the reading, odds are you'll struggle. Luckily, there's hope. Break the reading into shorter, bite-size chunks. Use a bookmark or paperclip to separate the text into milestones—5, 8, 10 pages at a time—whatever works for you. At each milestone take a break, do a dance, or eat something delicious. Then begin again and repeat until you're done. Breaking your long reading projects down into manageable goals will help you to stay motivated and focused.

TRICK: USE AN ENERGY BOOST

If you already don't enjoy reading, then a long reading assignment can be a drag. If your energy is lagging it can be doubly difficult. One suggestion is to use a natural energy boost from time to time. You might want to try some physical activity. A couple of jumping jacks or running in place can help to get your juices flowing. Or maybe a little snack might give you the energy you need. If all else fails and you really feel your eyelids drooping, a cold shower might be just the thing to wake you up. A natural energy boost will fuel you to conquer that long reading assignment with ease.

CHALLENGE: BOREDOM

We know many students find reading boring at times but this seems to be a much bigger problem for students with ADHD. Thankfully, the Homework Squad has come up with skills to help beat the boredom blues.

TRICK: ASK QUESTIONS AND MAKE PREDICTIONS

You'd give your right arm to be anywhere but in your seat reading. You find nothing interesting, not one nugget. You're questioning your teacher. You're questioning the world! Good. Now turn your questioning to the reading. Ask yourself questions about the material. Where is the author going with this? What will happen at the end? Then, after you have a list of questions, try to predict the answers and see if you're correct. Questioning and predicting are active reading strategies that make reading like a game you can beat or a puzzle you can piece together. Are you up to the task?

TRICK: BE THE CHARACTERS

A great technique to beat the boredom blues is to use character voices—in your head or out loud, whatever suits you! Imagine your favorite actor, athlete, friend, or goofy aunt reading the material to you. The voice of a character might just make that boring passage not so boring.

MATEO

When I found out this trick could keep me from getting bored, I became a huge fan. I love creating voices anyway, and now I've realized the sillier the character, the better!

TRICK: DIG FOR NUGGETS

We don't always have the freedom to choose what to read. One technique to beat boredom is to claw for something—ANYTHING!—about the material that interests you. Find that nugget of fun and relate the rest of the material to it. Say you're reading about the Revolutionary War and it's a total bore. Imagine that instead of the Colonies versus the British Empire, it's the two battling factions from your favorite fantasy game! You can raise the stakes, too. Pretend they're fighting over a magic crystal that teleports you to another dimension! That's more like it. Dig up something enjoyable, even if it's small, and you're more likely to remember the reading.

TRICK: GET A LITTLE HELP FROM YOUR FRIENDS

You've given reading a real effort, but nothing seems to work. You were born with a wicked case of the hate-to-reads. If so, your prescription is to make reading social. Join (or start) a book group that meets once a week to discuss the class reading. Add a fun element to the group like delicious snacks or games (or dogs!). The reading comes alive when you discuss it with friends.

CHALLENGE: SILENCE

Most students find it helpful to read in silence. The same is true for many ADHD learners who do well in a distraction-free setting. But for some of us, silence can ROAR! If you are anything like us, try these Homework Squad skills.

TRICK: TRY BACKGROUND NOISE

Pumping a little background noise into your earlobes can tame the silence lion, helping you read more efficiently and retain more information. Shiff told us many of the students he works with actually find it easier to focus on their reading material with some sound in the room. But background noise, such as music with words, can be distracting. Try music without words, like jazz or classical music. A white-noise machine can also work well. The key is to find a non-distracting sound. A tiny serving of background noise might be just the trick you need to stay focused.

TRICK: LISTEN TO AN AUDIOBOOK

Some of us are better auditory learners. That means we learn better with our ears. If you're an auditory learner, ask your teacher or librarian if there's an audio version of your book. You can also check online (Audible is a good place to start). For maximum comprehension, and a fun theatrical experience, combine both learning styles—visual and listening. As Shiff told us, the more ways you absorb the material, the better off you'll be. Therefore, reading along while you listen might just be your best bet.

 PRISHA

I couldn't agree more. This trick keeps my mind and eyes focused, so I can keep my wandering mind at bay.

TRICK: BE THE NARRATOR

If your book is not available as an audiobook, no sweat—YOU become the narrator! Use your own voice to dictate the reading into a recording device such as a smartphone. When you record your voice, you read the material once when you dictate it, and afterwards you can listen to it over and over again until it's stuck in your memory. It's the strangest thing, but something about hearing our voices helps us focus.

JOURNAL PROMPTS

Pick up any book you like and set a piece of paper beside it. When you get to the end of the chapter, think back on what you've read. Now, draw an illustration that represents it.

1. Did you find it easy or difficult to draw what you read?

2. Look at your illustration. Do you think you could use it to help you study what you read?

3. If you had another chance, would you draw something different?

Along with reading, many students with ADHD struggle with mathematics. Math requires a great deal of concentration and focus. A missed math step or two can lead to a failure to comprehend the material. And because a lack of focus is an issue most ADHD students struggle with, math can be very difficult. Some of the biggest math difficulties students like us struggle with are: remembering math facts, careless mistakes, word problems, time management, and a lack of focus. Luckily, the Squad has come up with a bunch of tricks that will hopefully help you reach your math potential.

CHALLENGE: REMEMBERING MATH FACTS

Are you one of those students who struggles to remember their math facts? You're not alone. This is a common problem for many students with ADHD. Luckily, the Squad has your back. Just try the tricks below.

TRICK: USE A MODEL

The Squad found that a good way to remember how to do certain types of math problems is to use a model. You can use a problem from your textbook, or an example your teacher has given you, as a template. Keep it in front of you and simply plug in the right numbers until you've mastered it. Eventually it will become second nature and then, BAM!—you've got it!

MICHAEL

I find this trick helpful because it's like working out how to win a game on the court—you've got to plug the right players into the right spot. Having a correct example to refer to also keeps me from getting discouraged.

TRICK: MNEMONICS (PRONOUNCED "NI-MON-IKS")

Another great trick for remembering your math facts is to use a mnemonic. This is a memory strategy that can help you remember a lot of different things. So why not apply it to math as well? You can use PEMDAS to help you remember the order of operations (Parentheses, Exponents, Multiplication, Division, Addition and Subtraction). Or how about Dumb Monkeys Sell Bananas to remember the steps for division (Divide, Multiply, Subtract, Bring down the next number).

Use your imagination to make up some of your own.

MATEO

I make up a mnemonic and then tell everyone at lunch. For me, the funnier the mnemonic, the easier it is to remember it.

TRICK: FORMULA CARD

The Squad found that another great way to help students with ADHD remember their math facts is to use note cards. Take each formula you are trying to remember and write them individually on note cards...otherwise known as "formula cards." Then use the cards to repeatedly test yourself until you have the formula memorized.

TRICK: CATCHY TUNE

If you're a musical person, a catchy tune can really help your memory. It can work for all subjects...including math. Whether you're trying to remember the steps to a specific formula, or the reasoning behind a mathematical concept, putting the words to music can improve your memory and understanding.

TRICK: EVERYDAY MATH

One way to enhance your memory for math facts and concepts is to use them in everyday situations. When possible, try applying the concepts around the house, at the park, in the grocery store, and in any real-world environment you can think of. For example, you can look for different patterns in your house such as the tiles on the floor or the panes in a window. You could then count how many of the items are across and down to practice your multiplication facts. The more you practice, the more likely you are to remember the material and enhance your math performance.

TRICK: MAKE A TABLE

If you're having a hard time remembering numbers, put them into an organized table. Organizing your numbers into a table will add structure, which enhances memory and retention. For instance, a multiplication chart allows you to easily find the product by bringing your fingers to one point where two numbers meet. Ask a teacher or parent to help you draw a grid. Write in the numbers 1–10 both across and down on the outside boxes. Then, fill in the numbers with their corresponding products.

TRICK: UNDERSTANDING THE MEANING

Many students with struggles similar to ours just don't like math. Most of us just try to get through our math work as quickly as possible because it feels like pulling teeth. Unfortunately, this just makes it worse: you're not really learning the material, which makes it harder to remember. We suggest taking a few extra minutes to really understand the reasoning behind your math problems. Try to go beyond memorizing the steps; get to the bottom of the equation and figure out why each step was necessary. This understanding helps you to remember it for the long haul.

TRICK: CALCULATE YOUR WAY TO SUCCESS

For some students with ADHD it is difficult to remember math facts. Think you can relate? Your parents may be able to request the use of a calculator for certain types of math assignments and tests. By using a calculator, some students are better able to master the concepts behind their math problems without getting bogged down with the facts.

CHALLENGE: CARELESS MISTAKES

Due to the difficulties with focus and concentration most students with ADHD struggle with, they often make many careless errors. We know how frustrating it can be when you know how to do a problem but get the answer wrong only because of a silly mistake. Don't worry! The Squad has some tricks that just might help.

TRICK: IMMEDIATE CHECK

While it's always a good idea to check over your work, many students wait until the end of the assignment and then go back to the beginning to start their review. If you have the time, (like on a homework assignment, not a timed quiz) we suggest reviewing each problem immediately after it's completed. That way the problem will still be fresh in your mind and you'll be more likely to catch the mistake.

TRICK: COLOR THE SIGNS

Another way to avoid careless mistakes is to use different color highlighters or pens to color the math signs. For example, addition signs can be highlighted in blue, subtraction signs can be colored green, etc. But using a coloring system, you'll be able to focus more on what the problem is asking for and less likely to make a careless mistake.

PRISHA

I use this trick often because it allows me to combine my love for art and one of my favorite classes, math!

TRICK: TURN YOUR NOTEBOOK

Let's face it, a lot of students with ADHD might produce work that...well...is a bit on the messy side. This can lead to difficulty lining up your math problems which can result in careless mistakes. So how about rotating your notebook?! By having the lines in your notebook up and down (vertically) as opposed to across the page (horizontally) it makes it much easier to line up your work. Give it a whirl. It just might work for you.

CHALLENGE: WORD PROBLEMS

Shiff told us many of the students with ADHD he works with find word problems to be extremely challenging. Why? Because they contain all of the ingredients for us to struggle. Misreading words or missing important details can create huge problems. Here are some tricks to completing your next word problems with ease.

TRICK: REMOVE EXTRA INFO

Think of it this way. Most word problems are designed to try to throw you off your game. Once we know that, we can look at what info from the problem we can remove. If the word problem is about the distance between a school, the park, and a kid's home, we don't need to worry about the color of the kid's hair, what team is playing in the park, or the mascot of the school. Any extra information that doesn't pertain to the problem can be crossed out. Talk about a breath of fresh air! Just make sure you read the question carefully to understand what it's asking you to figure out.

HUNTER

I really like this trick because the less I have to think about, the better!

TRICK: MULTIPLY YOUR UNDERSTANDING

To understand what info is crucial to obtain the answer to the problem, you have to read the question over a few times. This will help you avoid misreading words or skipping over words. Go ahead and underline any aspects of the problem you think are important, or that you don't understand. Then ask your teacher to go over those sections of the problem.

CHALLENGE: TIME MANAGEMENT

One major problem student with ADHD have is finishing their work in a timely manner. You can get distracted, lose focus, need to get up and move around, and the next thing you know your assignment that was supposed to take 20 minutes has taken two hours. The Squad knows how frustrating this can be. How about trying some of the tricks below to slay the time management dragon.

TRICK: EVERY OTHER PROBLEM

If you can get your teacher's (or school's) permission, try doing every other problem on a homework sheet. That way you will still learn the mathematical concepts, but you won't be spending hours getting it done. If you think this could help you, it might be worth discussing it with your parents or teacher.

TRICK: STUDY BUDDY

Do you ever find yourself constantly off-task? Your mind wanders and the next thing you know you've lost 20 minutes of work time. Try working with a study buddy. You can do your math homework together and it will help keep you on track. Shiff says many of his students find this helpful even if they're working on different assignments. Simply working next to their study buddy helps keep them engaged on their work.

TRICK: EXTENDED TIME

It goes without saying that many students with ADHD run out of time when trying to finish their math tests, quizzes, or homework assignments. Similar to the "Every other problem" trick, if you can get your teacher's and school's permission, you may be eligible for extended time to finish these exams and assignments. A little extra time may just make all the difference.

TRICK: ASK FOR A TUTOR

Math is hard. There's no doubt about it. If your work is taking you two or three times as long as it should, it may be that your ADHD is making it hard to study effectively or get your homework finished. Ask someone for help if you are struggling to get your work done on time. Your parents, teacher, or guidance counselor can help you find a math tutor. The tutor may be an older student, another teacher, or even a babysitter. If this isn't possible, ask your teacher if they have time for a few minutes after school to help you. Sometimes a little helping hand is all we need.

CHALLENGE: LACK OF FOCUS

Lack of focus is a key issue for most students like us. And as we've mentioned, this can have a huge impact on your math work. So try a few of the tricks below to help you.

TRICK: MEDICATION

If you are taking medication to assist you with your ADHD, you've probably noticed there are peak times when your medication has the most impact. Because math is one of the subjects most negatively affected by a lack of focus, scheduling your math class when your medication is working to its optimal efficiency might help. Ask your parents if they can speak to your school about arranging a schedule to fit your best focus times.

TRICK: USE MANIPULATIVES

Using manipulatives (objects that can be held or touched), such as dried beans or uncooked pasta, in math can have several benefits. First, it can help you learn the material. And secondly, because manipulatives are novel, they can help you stay focused on the task at hand.

 HUNTER

I like to work with dried beans because it keeps my hands and eyes focused on the problem. It also helps me remember the information later when it's test time.

So, try using these objects to assist with your math work whenever possible. They might just be more helpful than you think.

TRICK: TECH GAMES

Like using manipulatives, using technology, such as computer games, apps, etc., can be helpful with your math work. For example, with a quick trip to Google, or a quick app search on your phone, you can find cool quizzes, flash cards, games, worksheets, and a host of other math resources. Because many kids like using technology, it can lead to increased focus and retention.

JOURNAL PROMPTS

Take out your notes from your last math class. Color each math sign with a different color highlighter. Now, review the problem and find the solution.

1. Was it easier to read?

2. Was it easier to see each part of the problem?

3. Did you finish the math problem faster?

4. Would you use this trick in the future?

CHAPTER 3
WRITE YOUR HEART OUT

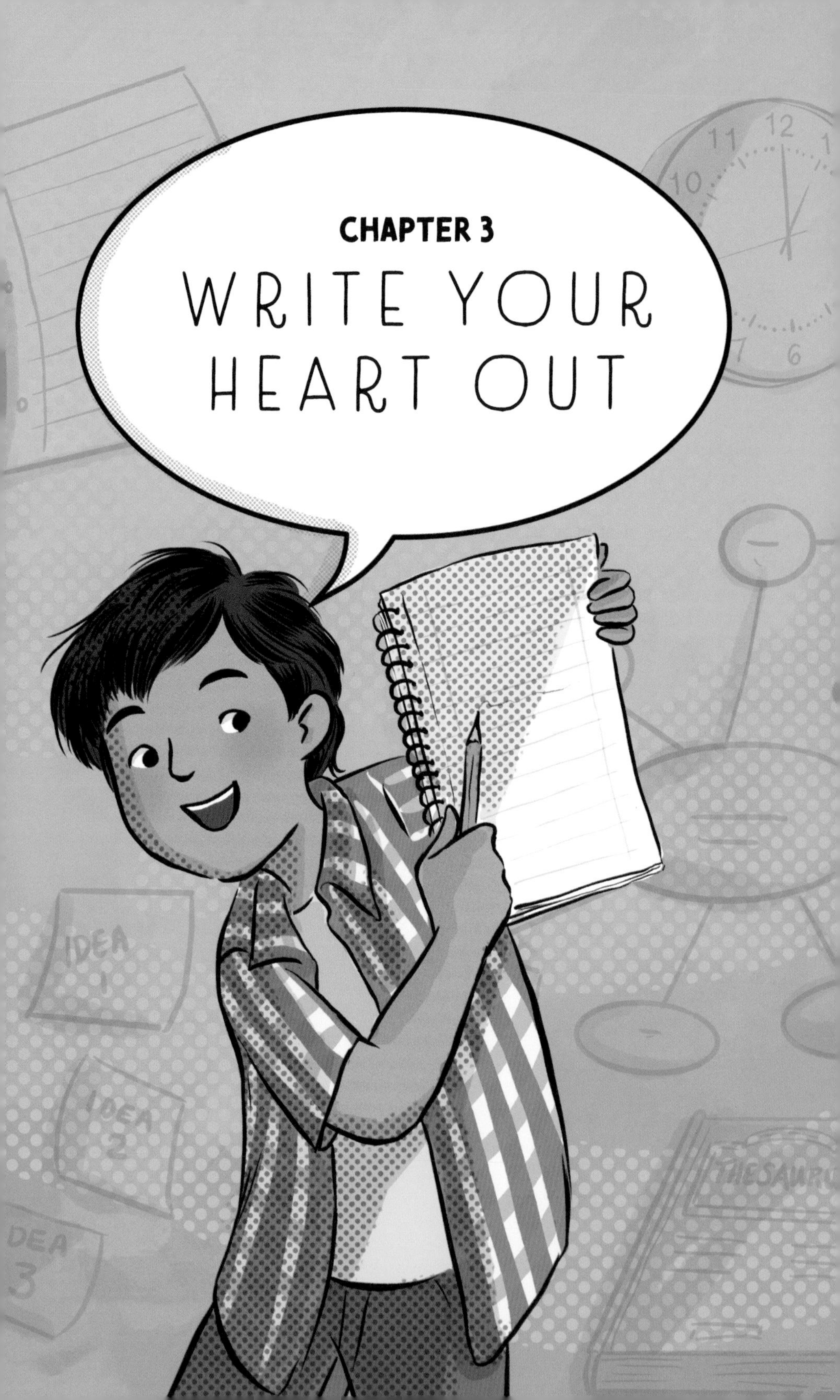

Writing is something we are all asked to do almost every day. And being a good writer is not only important for school, but for success in life as well. Unfortunately, if you're reading this book, you probably know that many students with ADHD struggle with writing. So, the Squad got together to come up with a list of writing challenges. They are time management, decision-making, getting your thoughts on paper, and slow writing. Never fear! We are confident you can improve your grades and your ability to write well with the tricks below.

CHALLENGE: TIME MANAGEMENT

While time management is a constant problem for many students with ADHD, it can rear its ugly head most often while writing. How much time do we need for writing, editing, and reviewing? It can all get overwhelming. At the end of the day, time management in relation to writing is all about practice. The more we do it, the better we become at understanding how much time we need. Even then, it's important to remember there are just some days when time is not on our side. Don't give up.

TRICK: ASK FOR EXTRA TIME

You may see this trick pop up throughout this book as a way to manage many challenges you face. That's because kids with ADHD usually have difficulty with time management and consequently, need more time for tasks. If time management is something you struggle with, it most likely negatively affects your writing as well.

MICHAEL

I used to always worry about running out of time, but now I know solving this problem is as simple as asking for more of it.

We suggest talking to your parents and teachers about the possibility of extra time on writing assignments and tests. It may just be the secret to your writing success.

TRICK: ONLY EDIT AT THE END

Stuck on a word? Don't let it interrupt your thought process. If we stopped at every word we couldn't spell correctly, we'd never finish a sentence! The editing process can, at times, seem to take longer than the actual writing itself. Well, remember those mnemonics we talked about in Chapter 2? We've come up with a couple that can help you with editing. We suggest putting the following two mnemonics to good use. COPS (Capitalization, Organization, Punctuation, Spelling) or C-SOOPS (Capitalization, Sentence Structure, Organization, Overall format, Punctuation, Spelling).

 MATEO

This helps me remember how to proceed with editing once I'm finished writing something. I don't lose time with spelling as I think up a creative story, and I know where to start when it's time to edit.

CHALLENGE: DECISION-MAKING

One of the most difficult challenges students like us have while writing is figuring out what to write about. Or, once we have a topic, how to get our thoughts on paper. Here are some tricks to help.

TRICK: BRAINSTORMING

Do you get stuck at the beginning of the writing process? Do you have difficulty coming up with a topic sentence, or even a general topic for that matter?

 HUNTER

For me, the beginning is the hardest part! That's why I really enjoy brainstorming because it focuses my mind and clears it of other distractions.

Just sit down at your computer, or with a big piece of paper in front of you, and write down whatever comes into your mind. After you have a bunch of ideas in front of you, it will be easier to choose the best one to write about.

TRICK: GRAPHIC ORGANIZER

If you have a topic but can't seem to organize your thoughts and ideas, try using a graphic organizer, otherwise known as a "Web Diagram" or "Mind Map." Write the main topic down in the middle of the page and then write supporting information in the area around the main topic. Another suggestion is to construct your Graphic Organizer like you would an outline by listing the main ideas, and then the supporting details in the order in which they will occur underneath. This will help you organize your ideas into a thoughtful, well-constructed essay.

TRICK: USE STICKY NOTES

Sticky notes are great because you can use them to organize the stuff that's jumbled in your brain. The advantage of using sticky notes is that they are rearrangeable. So, get all your ideas written on their own sticky notes, then feel free to reorder them as your ideas grow and change. Once you have everything in place, you can attach your sticky notes securely and start writing!

CHALLENGE: GETTING YOUR THOUGHTS ON PAPER

Many students with ADHD are very creative. A lot of them have all sorts of good ideas for a writing assignment, but have difficulty getting their thoughts on paper. Perhaps some of the tricks below will help you!

TRICK: YOU TALK—THEY WRITE

Ask an adult (or a friend who types or writes well) for help. As you speak, have your assistant write down what you're saying. It will speed up the process and might just lead to a successful paper.

TRICK: TOPIC SENTENCE HELP

Some students who struggle with writing can actually write pretty well, they just have difficulty getting started. Why don't you try thinking of a topic and maybe even use one of the aforementioned ideas (such as a graphic organizer) to get your thoughts on paper. Then, show your ideas to a parent or teacher and have them help you with a topic sentence or two. Once you get a topic sentence or two under your belt, it's easier to get the rest of your ideas rolling on the keyboard.

TRICK: USE A THESAURUS

ADHD or not, some students have great ideas, but struggle to find the right words. An easy solution is to use your thesaurus. For example, if you're looking for a different word than "good," by applying this trick you might find that "acceptable," "excellent," "favorable," "great," "positive," or a multitude of other words might just be a better fit. Instead of "nice," a quick search might help you come up with, "friendly," "kind," "lovely," etc. By opening up your actual hardback thesaurus, or more likely using the one on your computer, you'll be able to find just the right words to make your writing stand out.

CHALLENGE: SLOW WRITING

Shiff told us many students with ADHD struggle with the physical act of handwriting. These students grapple with slow, messy writing. Sound like you? Then try some of these tried and true Squad tricks.

TRICK: USE A COMPUTER

This trick is one you are probably using a lot at home, but may not be using in school. Many students who write slowly are actually quick at typing. Ask your parents if they can contact your school to request an allowance for your use of a laptop. It might make a world of difference.

TRICK: SPEECH RECOGNITION TECHNOLOGY

Here's another great trick that might help if you write slowly: speech recognition software. You know the routine. You speak and the computer types for you.

PRISHA

This works great for me because I can draw my ideas on paper while I talk about them into a microphone. The story I draw inspires what I write.

If this sounds like something you might benefit from, ask your parents or teacher if you can access this software.

JOURNAL PROMPTS

Pick a writing prompt. Maybe you already have one from school you can use. Sit down with a blank piece of paper and a pen, or at a computer. It's time to brainstorm! Write whatever comes to your head. Combine it with pictures. Cross things out. Circle what you like. Don't worry about how it looks. This is your time to get the creative juices flowing. See if you can do this for 15 minutes straight. When you finish, take a step back.

1. Do you feel like you now know what you want to write about?

2. How did it feel to have to focus for those 15 minutes?

3. Did you get distracted, did you become frustrated, or did you enjoy it?

4. Would you like to use this as a way to start writing going forward?

We don't know about you, but we find listening almost impossible—whether our math teacher is explaining prime numbers, or our parents ask us to take out the trash. Half the time, we're just not paying attention, and the other half, we swear we hear the words, but the information doesn't sink in! If this sounds like you, we are happy to report you are not alone! Whether you have ADHD or not, listening is a skill everyone in the world can work on. The Squad had a chat about the biggest challenges we face when it comes to listening, and these came out on top: paying attention to the speaker, remembering what was said, not getting distracted by other things, and finally, not falling asleep (what can we say, it happens!). And—you guessed it—we researched a bunch of tricks to help even the most distractible kids listen well.

CHALLENGE: PAYING ATTENTION

How many times do you hear this from an adult: "Please pay attention!" If only it were that easy. It turns out paying attention to what someone is saying can be extra difficult for kids with ADHD. Shiff says if all kids have a short attention span, kids with ADHD have one that's half as long. Imagine your brain is set on a conveyor belt. It can actively pay attention until it gets to the end of the belt. For some kids, the belt is as long as a basketball court. For kids with ADHD, it could be as short as a checkers board! Luckily with practice, you can learn to stretch your brain's conveyor belt so that it's the length of a football field! How, you might ask? The Squad has you covered.

TRICK: VISUALIZE IT

Listening can be downright hard for kids with ADHD. To make it a lot easier, try forming pictures in your head of what the speaker is saying. If your social studies teacher is giving a lesson on the ancient Egyptians, visualize a pyramid in your head as they talk. Imagine the Egyptians' faces, their makeup, the jewelry they wore. All the images you form in your head can keep you focused on what you are learning. Before long, you'll have an entire picture book on the Egyptians in your mind.

PRISHA

You better believe this works well for me. I take it a step further by drawing what I visualize. It's a great trick for paying attention, and a fantastic method to help me recall the lesson later on.

TRICK: LOOK 'EM IN THE EYE

How often do you really maintain eye contact with your teacher when they're speaking? Does it make you feel uncomfortable to look straight into their eyes? Us too. But that shouldn't stop us from learning! If you don't like eye contact, focus instead on the space right between their eyes. We promise, no one will be able to tell the difference. You'll stay focused while they talk and pay attention to what they are saying. On top of that, it's just the polite thing to do.

TRICK: WATCH THEIR MOVEMENTS

Okay, eye contact is great and all, but what happens if your teacher isn't staying put and you can't hold eye contact? You aren't an owl with a spinnable head! Not to worry. You can pay attention to what your teacher is saying by focusing on their movements. When your teacher speaks, what are they doing with their body? Are they gesturing with their hands? How are they physically expressing themselves as they teach? We can learn a lot about what someone is saying and how they feel when they say it by watching their body language. Is your teacher smiling while they talk? Are they frowning? Do they look sad, happy, frustrated, or serious? These are all cues that can help you pay attention to improve your listening skills.

TRICK: SHARE A SECRET CODE

Some kids with ADHD (Me! Me! Me!) interrupt a lot. It's not that we mean to be rude; we just find it hard to stay silent. There are plenty of things you can do. Shiff suggests letting your teacher know this is a challenge you face and asking if they can help. Often, teachers will create a silent code, such as touching their nose, or a quick tap on your desk, that will remind you to zip your lips.

CHALLENGE: REMEMBERING THE INFO

Just like reading, listening requires us to not only hear the words someone is saying but also to retain the information they've said. For those of us with ADHD, this can be an incredibly frustrating task, like I-want-to-pull-my-hair-out frustrating. Luckily for us, there are tons of tricks to remember information. Shiff says it's important to keep in mind that not every trick works for every kid. But by trying them out, you can see what works best for you.

TRICK: MAKE A WORD

Using acronyms is a great way to remember information, especially if you must recall the facts later on. For example, if your teacher is giving a lesson on the five Great Lakes, you can make a word out of the first letter of each lake to remember them better: HOMES (**H**uron, **O**ntario, **M**ichigan, **E**rie, **S**uperior). Voila! You can also practice your retention skills by using tricks like rhyming and writing songs.

TRICK: CREATE A STORY

Earlier, we talked about visualizing what your teacher is saying to improve your listening skills. Here, try creating a full story in your head about what the teacher is saying as a trick to remember the critical information. Let's use the ancient Egyptian example again. Instead of just visualizing the pyramids, make up a story about a young Egyptian you could relate to. Perhaps the Egyptian's parents were on the afterlife committee, or the young Egyptian spent their time making inscriptions because art was their favorite class in school. Whatever works.

Mateo

I do this all the time. Just be careful not to make the story so funny that you end up laughing out loud during a teacher's lesson (not that it's happened to me or anything!).

TRICK: WRITE IT DOWN

While it's great to watch your teacher the whole time they're talking, some of us retain information better by writing down the essential facts. As your teacher speaks, jot down the basic points. It's a great way to practice note-taking, and it gives your brain another chance to lock in what your teacher is saying. It also helps you practice registering the most important information. If you find this hard at first, you are not alone. It takes practice, so don't give up!

TRICK: REPEAT IT BACK

No, we are not talking about interrupting. But when your teacher takes a pause, a breath, or asks if there are any questions, this is your chance to raise your hand. When they call on you, repeat back what you heard them say and finish by asking a question. This trick serves two purposes: by repeating the information, you implant the facts a little deeper in your brain, and by asking a question, you keep yourself engaged in the lesson. For example, if your language arts teacher is explaining that "a lot" is actually two words, not one, you can raise your hand and say: "You said that 'a lot' is two words, not one, but what about when you say it really fast in a sentence?" Turns out, it's still two words, but remember, every question is a good question. So, ask away!

CHALLENGE: FALLING FOR DISTRACTIONS

Listening can be hard when there are so many things around to distract us. When someone is talking, we find it difficult to close off our eyes, ears, and nose to everything around us. That being said, there are tricks to keep our senses in check. While teachers can help, it's up to you to take responsibility for the things you know distract you. Here's what works for us.

TRICK: CHOOSE THE RIGHT SEAT

No, we aren't talking about the one by the window, or the door, or in the back of the classroom by your best friend. The best seat to decrease distractions and improve listening is the one closest to the teacher, most likely smack dab in the center of the room. We know, who wants to sit there, right? But try it, and you'll quickly see how much easier it is to focus on what your teacher is saying without being distracted by the squirrel climbing the tree outside, or your friend doing pretty much anything you find more interesting than your lesson.

TRICK: CLEAR YOUR DESK

If you are allowed to have a phone or a game in class, turn it off and get it out of sight. Otherwise, you are just asking for trouble. It is more fun to look at what is on your desk than listen to the teacher, but this doesn't just disrupt your brain, it disrupts the entire class. Leave your devices in your locker, or better yet, at home!

TRICK: WRITE A NOTE

By placing a simple note on your desk, you can have a constant reminder to pay attention. It can be as simple as writing "QUIET" on a piece of paper and taping it to the corner of your desk. You can even write down your favorite tricks from this book!

 HUNTER

I would be lost without my desk notes. I have one for each distraction that bothers me during the day, and it really works!

TRICK: FIND YOUR STRENGTH

Exercise helps us expend energy. When we don't get enough physical activity, our brains can go into over-drive, which makes it much more difficult to listen to instructions. Physical activity helps balance things out. We understand you may not like running or soccer, but perhaps you like playing capture the flag or skipping rope. Every day, it's important for kids to get at least an hour of exercise, ideally outside. Find what works for you!

CHALLENGE: STAYING AWAKE

Another big challenge ADHD kids face when it comes to listening is staying awake. How can we learn if we aren't awake? But how do we keep ourselves awake when it's so much easier to fall asleep? Shiff told us that small, simple changes can play a huge role in improving our energy levels and alertness. Here are a few of our favorite tricks to stay awake and listen well.

TRICK: EAT THE RIGHT BREAKFAST

Eating breakfast is the most underrated trick in the book! Our brains are muscles, and we need to keep them growing. Eating a healthy breakfast within 30 minutes of waking up is the best way to keep your brain happy, alert, and focused all day long. High-protein foods (like eggs), healthy fats (like avocados), and complex carbs (like oatmeal) are all fantastic options. Crave something sweet? Grab a piece of fruit or a handful of berries. And remember, don't eat too much sugar because you'll crash by the time your bus arrives at school!

TRICK: DRINK MORE WATER

Water keeps us alive and kicking, but sometimes we forget to drink enough of it. If we get dehydrated, we become sluggish, tired, forgetful, and, you guessed it, terrible listeners.

MICHAEL

I know how being hydrated affects me on the court, and I am a firm believer in the power of water. In fact, you won't see me without my sidekick water bottle. I fill it up once in the morning, and it's empty by the end of the day. That's how I can be sure I'm drinking enough water. If you don't have a water bottle, don't worry. Just be sure to go to the water fountain between classes.

TRICK: SLEEP LIKE A BABY

It may sound like common sense, but sleep and rest are crucial for listening and learning well. Kids require 9–10 hours of sleep every night. If you are not getting that, you can bet it will be pretty hard for you stay awake in class. Try to go to bed at the same time every night. If you have a hard time falling asleep, try reading a book or telling yourself a story. We talked about getting 60 minutes of physical activity before. While exercise gets us stronger and faster and healthier, it also helps us sleep better at night, so there's another reason to get outside and play!

JOURNAL PROMPTS

In your next class, if you don't have assigned seating, get there first and pick a seat in the front row. Use the experience to pay close attention.

1. Do you find you listen better?

2. Journal what you think was the most advantageous part about sitting in the front row.

3. Did anyone make fun of you for sitting in front?

4. Do you care?

5. Will you do it again?

Shiff has a few favorite sayings, one of them being: "Believe it, and you will achieve it." Sounds a bit corny, but it works. Setting a goal and working toward it is the first step to studying effectively. Kids like us can have some problems with goal setting, however, like setting expectations, staying positive, and challenging yourself. Hopefully, the Squad's tricks will get you on the path to success.

CHALLENGE: SETTING EXPECTATIONS

There's always room for improvement. Whether it's your favorite sport, a video game you like, or your ability to stop procrastinating, you can always get better. But you have to be fair and honest with yourself. Sometimes, to take a couple of steps forward you need to take one step back. Using a couple of the tricks below can help you manage your expectations.

TRICK: BEND LIKE A WILLOW

You're ready to work at your desk, and then sometimes life throws you a curveball. Your mom or dad will ask you to help them for a minute. Or the assignment may be more difficult than you anticipated. It can be enough to make you want to give up. The Squad suggests going with the flow. Take life's punches and keep going. Don't let a little setback completely throw you off track. Adjust your schedule as necessary and realize most things don't always go according to plan. Look at the challenge of rearranging things like a puzzle. How can it fit together correctly? Try thinking of yourself as a willow tree that will bend in a breeze but won't break.

TRICK: BE REALISTIC

Let's say that up to this point, school hasn't exactly been your thing. You've struggled with your work in the past and your grades have suffered. Perhaps that's one of the reasons why you are reading this book. While it doesn't hurt to shoot for the stars, we suggest being realistic with your goals. It may not be possible to get straight A's right away, but don't let that get you down and stop you from trying. Write down a few goals that seem unattainable (for instance, straight A's). You can call them stretch goals. Then, right down a few goals that seem attainable (not forgetting your homework this week). You can call these reach goals. Even a small improvement is something to celebrate.

TRICK: ENJOY THE JOURNEY

Life and school can be hard, especially with ADHD. Sometimes, things get so difficult that we don't even want to try. Look for the small victories and find enjoyment in the journey. If you end up being a straight-A student, good for you. Even if you see some improvement, our guess is you'll notice your motivation to keep doing better and your satisfaction with your efforts improve. Take the time to smell the roses and relish the small victories.

TRICK: BE PRECISE

Make sure your goals are precise, aka specific. Shiff says the more specific our goals are, the more likely we are to achieve them. So instead of saying, "I want to do well in English class," say, "I want to finish all my reading assignments, turn in all my homework, and score above a B- on all my essays." Measure and track your progress over short periods of time (days, weeks, school term). If you meet all your precise goals, chances are you'll find yourself succeeding in bigger ways, too.

CHALLENGE: STAYING POSITIVE

Have you ever heard someone say, "It all starts with the right attitude"? Well trust us, it's true. A positive attitude can really help you in school and in life. So, try these tricks to help keep your head up.

TRICK: DON'T BEAT YOURSELF UP

It can be easy to beat ourselves up. Sometimes we are our own worst enemy. Shiff says it always amazes him how people can be so hard on themselves. So instead of feeling upset that you are not the best student in class, try giving yourself the same advice you might give to a friend who came to you with the same problem.

 HUNTER

I fall into this pattern quite often. So now, instead of getting angry at myself, I write down three pieces of advice I would give a friend in the same situation. You might be amazed how a little positive self-talk helps you achieve your goals.

TRICK: SEEK ALTERNATIVES

So you're having a hard time reaching your goal. You have a plan that you've thought long and hard about, but it just isn't panning out. Don't give up! Try an alternative way to reach your goal. Having trouble reading your book? Look for an audiobook. Having difficulty writing your paper? Ask your teacher if you can give an oral presentation. As Shiff often says, "There's more than one way to get to the top of the mountain." Be creative, and you'll get there!

TRICK: USE POSITIVE WORDS

Sometimes achieving your goal is all about how you phrase it. Shiff says by stating your goals positively, as opposed to negatively, you're more likely to accomplish them. Instead of saying, "I don't want to fail," say, "I'm going to pass." Instead of saying, "I don't want to do poorly in school," try "I want to get an A or a B."

 MICHAEL

I try to use this advice whenever possible. I tell myself to stay positive. And it seems to work for me! By stating things positively, you'll be more likely to enjoy the sweetness of realizing your goal.

CHALLENGE: CHALLENGE YOURSELF

Anything worth accomplishing is going to take some effort. Whether you want to be the best basketball player like Michael, or a great artist like Prisha, you'll need to challenge yourself. We've talked a bit about stretch and reach goals, and it's important to have both. By challenging yourself with stretch goals, you are forcing yourself to continue to learn and grow. Remember, a lot of goals only seem unattainable until we try.

TRICK: LOUD AND PROUD

Many kids like us don't like setting goals because we have a hard time feeling ambitious. The Squad recommends you GET LOUD! Stand in front of a mirror, look yourself in the eye, and state your goals out loud until both you and your reflection believe you'll achieve them.

 MATEO

I do this every morning in a commander's voice. Probably because it makes me laugh, but also because it works! It's amazing how saying your goals out loud can help make them real.

TRICK: TELL SOMEONE

If you're having difficulty reaching your goals, it could mean you need more motivation. Believe it or not, telling someone really important to you about your goals, such as a parent, teacher, or friend, can help to motivate you.

PRISHA

This really helps me stay focused on achieving what I set out to do. I write down my goals at the beginning of the month and give them to my dad. He puts them on the bathroom mirror to remind us both what I have committed to.

The last thing you want is to let people know about your goals and then fail to accomplish them. Letting those close to you know about your goals might just give you the motivation you need to get across the finish line.

TRICK: MAKE IT WORTHWHILE

Some goals are fun to pursue. Others, simply put, are a pain in the you-know-what. While many students have a goal of studying harder and doing well in school, it can often be hard to encourage yourself to get there. At the Squad, we say make it worthwhile. Remind yourself why you've set the goal of improving your study skills, and why it's worthwhile to do so. Simply reminding yourself why your goals are worthwhile will likely help you reach a better outcome.

JOURNAL PROMPTS

Write down three stretch goals. One for the month, one for the term, and one for the year. Then, write down your answers to the following questions:

1. Does it scare you to think about these goals?

2. What are you most scared of about these goals?

3. What do you need to achieve these goals?

4. Who can you ask to support you in achieving them?

Taking good notes has tons of benefits. Not only can it help with studying and reviewing the material, but it can also help keep you engaged in what your teacher is saying. Note-taking can be especially difficult for the ADHD student because it splits our attention in two. It requires us to listen *and* write. Or to read *and* write. At the heart of note-taking is multitasking, which can be a challenge when you aren't great at focusing. Luckily, the Squad has come up with some tricks to solve the following challenges: keeping it clean, avoiding lazy habits, and getting all the notes you need.

CHALLENGE: KEEPING IT CLEAN

Have you ever tried to take notes, scribbling furiously during class, only to later realize they make no sense? Many kids like us struggle to take notes in general, and when we do the notes often end up looking like a mess. If this sounds like you, try these tricks to help keep your notes clean and clear.

TRICK: LAPTOP MAGIC

If you're a slow or messy writer, try bringing a laptop into class. Typing is so much faster than writing by hand! And you don't need to worry about messy handwriting or wrist cramps. Ask if you can use your laptop during class to keep up with the lecture and type notes you can actually read. We at the Squad have found teachers are usually pretty understanding if you explain why you need this assistance.

TRICK: REWRITE THE UGLY

Ever have trouble reading your own notes? Rewrite them as soon as possible after class. That way, you'll remember what you were trying to say and your notes will make more sense.

MATEO

This trick helps me remember what I've learned because it forces me to review it a second time as I rewrite it.

Take your time to rewrite the notes neatly and make sure they are understandable. Not only will you have good notes to review later, but rewriting everything will help reinforce what you learned.

TRICK: CODE BY COLOR

The Squad all agrees that when we go back to look over our notes it is a total snooze fest...SOOO boring. Shiff gave us a good trick to help bring our notes to life. He suggested using different colored pencils to write the different parts of our notes. For example, the general information would be in black. If something was really important, we would write it in red. If there was something we didn't totally understand and had to review later, we would write it in green. You can pick whatever colors work for you. Not only will this help you stay organized, but Shiff says studies have shown it helps your memory as well.

TRICK: SPACE THINGS OUT

As we said, many students with ADHD end up with messy notes that are hard to understand. One solution to this problem is to space out your notes. Don't cram all the words or drawings into one small area. Give yourself room on the page. It will be easier to read and if you want to add information later, you'll have the room for it.

CHALLENGE: AVOIDING BAD HABITS

We all have some bad habits. Whether it's biting our fingernails, being a couch potato, or eating too much junk food, nobody's perfect. Well, the same thing holds true for note-taking. The Squad has come up with a few tricks to help turn those bad habits into a winning formula.

TRICK: HAVE A PEN HANDY

Have you ever gotten to class only to realize you don't have a pen or pencil? It's textbook ADHD. You obviously can't take notes if you don't have anything to write them down with. So get into the habit of carrying a writing utensil with you whenever you are in school, at the library, or studying in general.

 HUNTER

For me, a pencil is like a skateboard—I always have it with me.

Try to find a pen or pencil that you really like. I know it sounds crazy, but in the Squad we all have our favorite type of writing device. Being prepared and ready with your writing weapon of choice is half the battle.

TRICK: DIVIDE THE PAGE

Many kids like us get into the bad habit of writing notes they never look at again. One way to avoid this is to write your notes on a divided page. Make a crease by folding your page in half from side to side (like a hotdog bun). Use the left side to write the terms you need to remember. On the right side, write the definitions. Then, when you are studying for the test, fold the page so you only see the terms. Practice defining them in your own words; then flip the page and read the definitions. This method will help you get the most out of your note taking.

TRICK: BEDAZZLE IT

A lot of us have trouble keeping our eyes on our notes. We get it—paper is boring! But what if your notebook was not boring? Decorate each page of your notebook with designs and crafts. (If you use a laptop, decorate that!) Color-code your pencils and use color highlighters.

PRISHA

I love this trick because it lets me use art to make note-taking more exciting.

Fun notebooks will make outside distractions less attractive and will help you keep your eyes on the paper.

CHALLENGE: GETTING ALL THE NOTES YOU NEED

Despite all the tricks above, you still might find yourself with incomplete notes. Sure, you may have done your best to write your notes neatly and to avoid some of the bad habits we discussed. Yet even with these extra efforts your notes still may not be up to snuff (that's what Hunter's grandpa says when he means something's not good enough). If you're someone who tries and tries but can't seem to write nicely, then you might benefit from the tricks below.

TRICK: REVIEW WITH YOUR TEACHER

If you feel like you've struggled to take adequate notes during a class, go right to the source. After class, or after school if necessary, go over your notes with your teacher and ask them for help. Your teacher should be able to tell you what you missed. This extra effort will also help you improve your notes in the future, as well as prove to your teacher that you are a serious student.

 MICHAEL

This is just like when I go for an extra workout at basketball. Both my coach and my teacher really seem to appreciate that I'm putting in the extra work...and, of course, it helps me improve as well.

TRICK: CHECK THE TEACHER'S NOTES

Ask your teacher kindly if they are willing to lend you a copy of their notes. That way, you can fill in any gaps in your own notes. Hint: this will probably work better if your teacher sees that you really tried to take your own notes first! If your teacher sees you are making a serious effort and trying your best, they just might go for it.

TRICK: ASK FOR A SYLLABUS

A syllabus is like an outline for the course. They are popular in high school and college, but some middle and elementary school teachers use them as well. If your teacher doesn't provide a syllabus, ask them if they can help you create one. A syllabus can help you prepare for what's coming up in class, and a more prepared student will be able to take more effective notes.

TRICK: FIND A NOTE BUDDY

We'd recommend this strategy even to strong note-takers, but especially to students like us. Find a good student in your class and ask them to swap notes every few days after school. You can use their notes to fill in the gaps in your work, and they can do the same. Even the best of note-takers ends up missing information from time to time. So finding a note buddy can help both of you...it's a win-win!

JOURNAL PROMPTS

Take out your notebook and look at your notes from yesterday. Now rewrite all of them.

1. How long did it take you?

2. Was it tiring?

3. Did it give you a better sense of what you learned?

4. How does it feel to be looking at clean and clear notes?

One of the main reasons kids with ADHD often struggle in school is because we lack effective study skills. It seems like it's way, WAY harder for students like us to study efficiently and successfully. This chapter focuses on staying organized, reviewing like a champ, and finding the right motivation. One of the best ways to get to the head of the class is to improve your study habits.

CHALLENGE: STAYING ORGANIZED

Overwhelmed by work. Assignments are late. Your schedule is a mess. Sound familiar? While this type of chaos might seem like a natural part of your everyday life, it doesn't have to be. One of the easiest ways to improve your ability to study is to stay organized. Don't believe us? Try some of the tricks below and watch as your ability to stay organized, and your grades, progress.

TRICK: USE A PLANNER

One of the worst feelings we all have is showing up to school and realizing there's a test we forgot to study for. An easy solution is to use a planner. Use your planner to list all assignments, both daily and long-term. Your planner should be small enough so you can take it everywhere with you. As soon as your teacher gives you homework to complete or tells you about a test, write it down in your planner immediately. Don't forget to check your planner several times a day. Getting in the habit of using a planner will help keep you on track and on top of your work.

MICHAEL

When I got my planner in order, I found it also helped declutter my brain. Don't ask me how that works!

TRICK: SET A DAILY SCHEDULE

Now that you have a planner set up, the next step is to use a daily schedule. The best way to do this is to set up your schedule each night for the next day. You should use your daily schedule for everything: when you plan to wake up, eat breakfast, get your work done, hang out with friends, etc. You'll also want to make sure not to overschedule yourself. Things often take longer than you think they will. By planning a daily schedule and sticking to it, you'll find that you end up being more productive and efficient, which will lead to better grades.

PRISHA

This works well for me. I love how much I can accomplish. And when I finish each task, it makes me really happy to cross it out and draw a little heart next to it.

TRICK: TIME EVERYTHING

As we mentioned in the previous trick, tasks for students with ADHD often seem to take longer than we originally planned. Your teacher may have told you that you should study for two hours for an upcoming quiz. You have the quiz written in your planner and on your daily schedule (good for you!), but when you get down to studying your mind starts to drift, you're out of your chair, and after the two hours have passed you realize that in reality you've actually only studied for about 20 minutes. Using a clock or stopwatch and monitoring your time can help keep you on track. Also set a timer or snooze button to go off periodically: if you aren't studying productively, it can help get you back to work.

TRICK: MAKE A WEEKEND SCHEDULE

The weekend is a time to relax and unwind. But sometimes you need to do a little work as well. If your teacher or school assigns work over the weekend, make a schedule to help plan out your activities. From our experience, if you just wing it and think you'll get your work done when you have a chance, you're likely to run into problems. Spend a few minutes on Friday after school planning out your weekend schedule. Don't forget to add sporting events, time with friends, and down time. Also remember to account for travel time and that many things take longer than anticipated.

CHALLENGE: TAKING TIME TO REVIEW

As Shiff told us many times, it doesn't matter how smart you are: if you want to do well in school, you have to put in the effort. One way to do this is to make sure you review your work. The Squad has come up with some tricks to make reviewing a bit easier.

TRICK: STUDY IN BITE-SIZED CHUNKS

There are so many studies on cramming and they all say the same thing: DON'T DO IT! This is especially true for students like us, who might have difficulty remembering information in the first place. Shiff told us if you want to study for four hours for a test, you are much better off studying an hour a night for four straight nights as opposed to trying to study for four straight hours the night before the test. By studying over time, you're more likely to retain the information and ace that exam.

TRICK: COMPLETE PRACTICE TESTS

When studying for an upcoming exam, it's always a good idea to review old material. If your teacher is nice enough to hand out a practice test, the Squad strongly suggests you take advantage of this and complete it. In almost every case, the questions on the practice exam will be similar to the ones on the real exam. If your teacher doesn't hand out a practice exam, then at least review the quizzes that came right before the exam, as there will likely be similar information. Sure, this might seem like a bit of extra work, but it's worth it.

TRICK: REVIEW AGAIN AT BEDTIME

Each night, before you go to sleep, it can be really helpful to review the material right before you put your head on the pillow and shut your eyes.

MATEO

I like this trick because it not only helps me the next day at school, it also gets me in the mood to go to bed. This gets my mind off everything else, and actually puts me into dream mode when I finish.

Shiff told us there is a lot of research on this topic. The results suggest that studying right before bedtime, regardless of the material, leads to better recall and memory. The result will be more effective studying with less effort...doesn't that sound great?

TRICK: USE FLASHCARDS

This is an oldie but a goodie. When reviewing your material, try writing a question on the front of a flashcard, and write the answer on the back. Then pull a card from the pile, answer it, and flip the card to check whether your answer was correct. Seems easy, right? Just make sure to review the flashcards randomly so you really know the answers and aren't just memorizing them in order.

CHALLENGE: FINDING MOTIVATION

We get that many students don't love studying. Wouldn't it be great if we could just hang out with our friends all day and do what we wanted? Unfortunately, that's not the way the world works. And to be honest, learning about new things...even in school...can be interesting. But the reality is many students struggle with their motivation, especially ones with ADHD who often find studying to be so difficult. But a little motivation can be the difference between success and failure. So the Squad has come up with some tricks to help you get off the couch and start working.

TRICK: CLEAR YOUR SCHEDULE

One reason many students with ADHD struggle with their motivation is because they have ten other things they would rather be doing. One good trick is to clear your schedule. Let your friends and family know that for a certain time each day you are not to be interrupted. Turn off your phone, tablet, television, and any other distracting device. Some students even like to put a "Do Not Disturb" sign on their door. Then go to your room, or the kitchen table, or wherever it is you do your most productive studying, and get to work. By clearing your schedule for a certain amount of time each day, you'll be amazed at how much more motivation you'll have to study more effectively.

 HUNTER

I find this super useful when my little sister, Jade, is running in and out of my room without warning. A sign on the door gives her a clear understanding that she can't bother me while I'm studying.

TRICK: CHOOSE YOUR TIME WISELY

Are you an early riser? A night owl? Do you hit your peak right after lunch? Most of us have a time of the day where we study most efficiently. If you are not sure when that is for you, do a little experimenting. Try studying at different times of the day to see what works best for you. After identifying the right time, try to schedule most of your studying during that period of the day. It's amazing how much more motivated you will be when studying at the right time for you. This is what the Squad likes to call "studying smarter, not harder."

TRICK: SET MILESTONES

When many of us get a big assignment, we don't even know where to begin. It can be so overwhelming that it's nearly impossible to start. This is especially true for students like us. Try setting some milestones and then give yourself a little reward when you conquer each step. For example, after reading a certain number of pages in a book, or after working on that science project for an hour or two, take a bite of your favorite food, or play video games for a few minutes. Setting manageable milestones and achieving them will further motivate you to keep going. Success leads to more success!

JOURNAL PROMPTS

Set a schedule for the week. Go through each hour of the day, from the moment you wake up to the moment you go to bed. Write down what you'll do, setting a specific time aside for studying each day. For example, you could write: 7am - wake up. 7:10 - shower. 7:30 -breakfast 7:45 - catch the bus...etc. Try to stick to your schedule and amend it if you find it doesn't work. Maybe you need more time studying and less time in the shower. At the end of the week, think back on your schedule.

1.   Were you more or less productive?

2.   Was it hard to stick to the schedule?

3.   Did you study every day?

4.   Did you remember to refer to the schedule?

5.   Was it hard to create?

If there's one thing we know students with ADHD struggle with, it's their ability to concentrate. A lack of focus is one of the key elements of ADHD. As we know from personal experience, getting lost in your thoughts or tangled in distraction is no fun. Start by *clearing the clutter*—inside and out. In this chapter, the Squad empowers you by helping you keep your eye on the prize, find your calm, and keep your momentum.

CHALLENGE: KEEPING YOUR EYES ON THE PRIZE

How do you keep your eye on the prize when you can't even keep your eyes on your paper? We get it. You know there's a reason you are meant to be paying attention in class or doing this homework, but sometimes that feels less important than absolutely anything else going on around you. So, how do you keep that end goal in mind? Here are a few tricks we've come up with.

TRICK: PUT IT ON THE CALENDAR

Let's say you have an assignment due at the end of the month. There's a lot of time between now and then to get distracted, twiddle your thumbs, or forget about it completely. Put it on the calendar so you won't lose track.

PRISHA

I don't just put the assignment's due date; I also put what I will feel when it is completed. When I can remind myself that it's about more than just handing the assignment in, I can stay focused and motivated to complete it.

TRICK: ASK YOURSELF QUESTIONS

To help keep your eye on the prize and focus, ask yourself a bunch of questions. What do I think is going to be the topic during class today? Where do I think the teacher is going with this lecture? Why do I think this is important? Then come up with answers in your head to each question, and try to see if you're correct. Playing this question game can help keep you on track and focused throughout the school day. And as a little extra benefit, the Squad has found we end up learning the material better, too.

TRICK: REDUCE SCREENS

Okay, we get it. This is a tough one. We all love our televisions, computers, phones, tablets, and video games. The problem is, studies have shown that too much screen time negatively affects focus and concentration. We're realists, though, and we know it's almost impossible to cut out screen time altogether. But if you can just try to limit it as much as possible, you might notice an improvement in your ability to focus. Why not give it a try?

CHALLENGE: FINDING YOUR CALM

Many great athletes, like our Squad member Michael, talk about being "in the zone." That's the place where they experience a kind of tunnel vision and are able to focus really well. One way to find the zone is to find your calm. It's where you feel relaxed and able to just be, which improves your ability to focus. With Shiff's help, the Squad has come up with several tricks to help you find your zone of calm.

TRICK: CLEAR YOUR MIND

Studies have linked things like meditation and yoga to improved focus and concentration. Take a few minutes to engage your "calm brain" before tackling tasks that require your powers of concentration. Sit comfortably. Breathe in deeply through your nose, not just into your chest, and let your stomach expand. Then exhale through your mouth, sending all tension rushing to your toes. Envision the tension leaving your feet and growing roots beneath you. Repeat these steps. A calm brain will help you relax and clear your mind, making you less susceptible to distraction or confusion.

 HUNTER

I like to meditate for a few minutes in the morning before the craziness of the day begins.

TRICK: USE SCENTED OILS

In the upcoming chapter on memorization, the Squad discusses how certain smells may be helpful for recall and retention. Well, believe it or not, if your parents can pop a scented oil into a diffuser, it may also help you find your calm and enhance your concentration. There are many scented oils that can be helpful. Some of the Squad's favorites include vetiver and cedarwood. If your parents don't own a diffuser to activate scented oils safely, you may be able to find scents naturally—think lavender, vanilla, rosemary, and mint. They can be found in a garden, your parents' flowerpots, or even in the grocery store. Ask your parents or teacher if they have access to any of the scents above.

TRICK: KEEP IT SPICK-AND-SPAN

We know from personal experience that many students with attentional difficulties have a messy workspace. This can make it very difficult to find your calm. It's really hard to concentrate when you're surrounded by leaning towers of books, wads of chewing gum wrappers, or mountains of dirty clothes. Make sure your study space is as clean and organized as you want your mind to be. If your study space is already clean, take five minutes to organize another room. It will get you in the productivity mindset—watch your powers of concentration skyrocket.

CHALLENGE: KEEPING THE MOMENTUM

Although they may seem few and far between, there are times when all of us study well. Perhaps we're interested in the material, or maybe it's because we have a big test the next morning and we're up against the clock. Regardless, when you're in the groove and studying well, you want to do your best to keep the momentum going. In these situations, try the tricks below to get you past the finish line.

TRICK: TAKE BREAKS

 **MICHAEL**

When I'm exercising, like playing basketball, after a while my muscles need a break. The same thing happens when I'm studying: I need to give my brain a break now and again to recover.

Shiff told us research suggests that after about 45–60 minutes of studying, you should take a 5–15 minute break. If you try to go much longer than an hour without taking a break, you won't be working at your best. Just make sure that 5–15 minute break doesn't turn into an all-day break. Take a few minutes to get a snack or do a few jumping jacks, and then get back to work.

TRICK: BREATHE

Another trick to break up the boredom blues is to take a deep breath from time to time. If you've been studying and feel yourself getting a little woozy, but you're not quite ready for an extended break, try taking a few deep breaths. Ideally you would inhale deeply through your nose and exhale through your mouth. A few deep breaths might just be the reset activity you need to push forward.

MATEO

I find this especially useful because I often get really tired when working. I puff my chest out like a superhero as I breathe, and it really works!

TRICK: STRETCH

If you feel a bit of fatigue coming on, take a second to get up and stretch. At the Squad we suggest getting up out of your chair and touching your toes, reaching for the ceiling, and then stretching a bit from side to side. You'll be amazed at how a little stretching can get the juices flowing and give you the energy to continue plowing ahead.

TRICK: BRING A SNACK

Sometimes we lose our focus because we get hungry. Or perhaps your blood sugar is a bit low, which can lead to a lack of concentration. And of course, a lack of focus can lead to your work taking longer than you expected. So, always carry a piece of fruit, a granola bar, nuts, or whatever sounds good to you. The next time you notice a dip in your concentration, perhaps a quick energy boost is all you need.

JOURNAL PROMPTS

Ask your parents or teacher for help finding a free online meditation practice specifically for kids. Afterwards, write down how it made you feel.

1. Did you like the meditation?

2. Did you become bored?

3. Did you fall asleep during it?

4. Was it what you expected?

5. What was the first emotion you could identify when you finished?

6. Did you want the meditation to go on longer than it did?

7. Would you try meditating again?

Where do answers go when you can't remember them? It's like the wind scoops them up and whisks them away. Memory isn't something we are born with. In fact, like many things, it's a skill that can only be improved upon through practice. Shiff told us training your memory is as important as eating because it is a skill we'll use throughout our life. The problem is, memorizing and ADHD go together like ketchup and chocolate cake...yuck! The truth is, kids with ADHD forget assignments, facts, and figures all the time. But, just like everything, we can improve our memory and reduce our forgetfulness little by little with these useful tricks the Squad put together for inside and outside the classroom.

CHALLENGE: FORGETTING ASSIGNMENTS

Isn't it frustrating when you forget to do your homework? You forgot to write it down or didn't hear the teacher assign it. Or how about this...you did your work and forgot to hand it in or left it at home...ugh! Try a few of the tricks below to hone your homework memory.

TRICK: KEEP ASSIGNMENTS IN ONE PLACE

One good trick to help you remember your work is to keep it all in the same place. It can be a certain spot on your desk, or in your notebook—wherever you'll remember to check it consistently. You might even want to put a note

on your bedroom door that says, "Check assignments."
By putting your homework in the same place every day,
you'll be more likely to remember it, do it, and turn it
in consistently.

 HUNTER

I now keep a clean and organized part of
my desk where I place all of my assignments
and so far I haven't forgotten to turn in my
homework, or more importantly, to study for
a test, even once!

TRICK: SET A REMINDER

A lot of students with ADHD are naturally forgetful. We
forget where we put our backpack, where our favorite
baseball cap is, or (of course) to do and hand in our homework. So set a reminder! It can be a sticky note on the
bathroom mirror, an alarm on your phone, or just asking
your parents to help you be less forgetful. A good system
can help keep you organized and on track.

TRICK: COMPLETE IT QUICKLY

Ever hear the expression, "out of sight, out of mind"? It
basically means that once you put something aside, you
forget about it. That's why it's a good idea to do your
homework as soon as you can. Don't put it off for later

when you are likely to forget about it. There is no time like the present.

MICHAEL

I made this trick a daily practice because it gives me more time to shoot hoops.

CHALLENGE: FORGETTING FACTS

Shiff taught us that ADHD can give us trouble with our "working memory." That's the part of the brain that holds onto information in your short-term memory. And if your working memory isn't working efficiently, then it's a challenge to get the information from your short-term memory into your long-term memory, where you can remember the information for the long haul. But don't worry. The Squad has come up with several tricks to help every student remember their facts more easily.

TRICK: CREATE A SONG

If you are musical, then this trick is for you. Make a song out of the information you are trying to remember. Whether it's about a battle in World War II, the state capitals, or the names of the presidents, if you are able to make up a song about the information, you'll be amazed at how your recall improves.

Mateo

I created a long list of songs on everything from U.S. capitals to secondary colors. If it works for me, maybe it will work for you, too!

TRICK: SAY IT OUT LOUD

Give voice to the facts. If you're in a place where you can't speak freely, such as a library, even whispering the words can increase your remembrance of them. If the whisper police tell you to shush, mouthing the words silently will do. This technique can be especially helpful with more difficult material you wouldn't normally talk about.

TRICK: USE ACRONYMS

Not so musical? How about trying an acronym? It works by making a word out of the first letter of longer words or phrases. You probably remember learning the colors of the rainbow by using the acronym "ROY G. BIV" for "red, orange, yellow, green, blue, indigo, and violet." Acronyms can be super helpful for a variety of different information you need to remember. For example, if you are trying to remember the order of your math operations you might try using the acronym "PEMDAS" which will help you remember "Parenthesis, Exponents, Multiplication, Division, Addition and Subtraction." Remember mnemonics from Chapter Two? Acronyms are a type of mnemonic device. You can also come up with a funny sentence to help you remember the acronym, such as "Please Excuse My Dear Aunt Sally" for "PEMDAS."

TRICK: JOT IT DOWN

If you struggle to remember information you learn, take short notes in a notebook or on a sticky note as you go along. This will not only help you remember the information, but it will also keep you engaged with the class by improving your ability to focus. For example, you just learned about how Albert Einstein worked in a patent office before he was famous. Your note might read: "Smart mustache dude = Einstein. Worked in patent office. Patents protect inventions." A jot here and a jot there will help improve your ability to concentrate and in turn get a lot more out of your learning.

TRICK: DRAW A PICTURE

If you're artistic, like Prisha, you might want to try drawing a picture that represents the material you are trying to remember. For example, drawing a picture of George Washington crossing the Delaware River to fight the Redcoats in the Revolutionary War can help you remember this historic battle.

 PRISHA

As I like to say, the more detail you add, the better.

TRICK: SMELL SWEET SMELLS

Do you have a favorite smell? Do you like lavender, the smell of certain candles, or other relaxing scents? Shiff told us your nose can affect your memory, so take advantage! Fill your study space with a pleasing aroma so you can focus better and remember more.

TRICK: REMEMBER YOUR FAVORITE ROAD

Think about a route you travel often—your walk home from school, perhaps. Let's say you need to memorize all the planets. Imagine Jupiter at the top of the tallest tree at school, Saturn in the middle of the traffic circle, Mars near your neighbor's red roses, and so on. Putting the info, you need to remember on top of a mental roadmap can help you recall long lists of information.

JOURNAL PROMPTS

When you study today, say or whisper everything you read aloud.

1. Does the concept sink in deeper?

2. Can you remember what you studied more easily?

3. How does it compare to studying without speaking?

4. Could this be the way you memorize facts in the future?

You've probably heard someone say, "I'm just not a good test taker. I study. I know the material. But when it comes to the test, I just can't do it." Test taking struggles are real. And they can be especially difficult for students with ADHD. But with Shiff's help, the Squad has come up with tricks that focus on concentrating on test questions, following directions, finishing on time, and scoring well to help you ace that exam.

CHALLENGE: CONCENTRATING ON THE QUESTIONS

It goes without saying that students like the Squad members have difficulty concentrating in many different aspects of their lives, and test taking is no exception. But by implementing a few easy tricks, the Squad can help you focus when it's most important (like when you're taking that big exam).

TRICK: CREATE THE SPACE

A lack of focus can be a pain in lots of circumstances, but during any sort of important assessment it can turn into a major issue. Ask your teacher if you can work in a quiet space that limits distractions. For some students, a quiet spot in the back of the classroom works well. For others, some sort of study carrel with dividers might do the trick. And for some students, working in the hallway might be the answer they're looking for.

Creating the right space is the first step toward working to your potential.

HUNTER

What works best for me is having a bit of room around without any distractions.

TRICK: SILENCE THE NOISE

Many students would have a hard time taking a test in a noisy atmosphere. If you're reading this book you probably realize that with ADHD, every little sound gets magnified. The ticking of the clock, the bird chirping outside, the classmate next to you tapping his pencil, it can all be too much at times. Finding a quiet space can help, but if that's not quite enough, try earplugs or noise-cancelling headphones. Sometimes a little silence can go a long way.

TRICK: REQUEST QUESTIONS ORALLY

Reading during an exam can be a struggle for any student because of the added stress of test-taking, but it is especially difficult for kids with ADHD. Don't worry, it's completely normal. Just ask your teacher if they can read the questions to you out loud in a private setting. Sometimes, hearing the questions that way can help with focus and lead to better results.

CHALLENGE: FOLLOWING DIRECTIONS

Kids with ADHD have a lot of different symptoms, but one that most ADHD students share is a lack of focus. This can be a big problem when directions are given during an exam. Whether the directions are given out loud or in writing, if you aren't able to follow the requirements of the assessment carefully, you'll be behind the eight ball from the start. If this has ever happened to you, try some of the Squad's best tricks to help you follow directions effectively.

TRICK: ASK YOUR TEACHER TO EXPLAIN THE DIRECTIONS IN A DIFFERENT WAY

What happens if you are really struggling to understand the directions on an exam? You've listened to the teacher and read the directions several times, but you're still uncertain about how to move forward. If Shiff has said it once, he's said it a million times: "You have to be willing to self-advocate." In other words, you have to be able to speak up when you need help.

 MICHAEL

The first time I asked for help it was scary, but once I discovered the teacher was happy to provide me with an alternative way of looking at the question, I realized how much I'd been missing by not asking sooner!

If you are really confused, go up to your teacher and ask them to explain the directions to you again, or in a different way so you make sure you understand what to do. The first step to doing well on any test or quiz is to fully comprehend the directions.

TRICK: LISTEN UP

We get it! It can be hard to concentrate for long periods of time with ADHD, especially if you find the material boring. But there are times when it really helps to give your best effort. When you know a test is about to start, tell yourself you're going to make every attempt to listen carefully to the directions. Your teacher will normally only spend a minute or two explaining what needs to be done. So, hang in there, sit up in your chair, focus your eyes on your teacher, and do your absolute best to listen up.

TRICK: REPEAT IT BACK

One last trick the Squad has found helpful for following test directions is to repeat back the information. For some students, that means saying the information back internally (saying it back to yourself silently). Some students, like us, find it helpful to subvocalize, or to whisper the directions back. And finally, other students find it helpful to raise their hand, and when called on, repeat the directions back out loud. The key to any of these methods is to try and repeat the directions in your own words while keeping the meaning the same. The Squad suggests, when possible, repeating the directions back out loud to the teacher.

This way your teacher can make sure you have the information right.

CHALLENGE: FINISHING ON TIME

Living with ADHD can be frustrating for a variety of reasons. And for us, one of the top struggles is running out of time on an exam. Even when we've studied and know the material backward and forward, when the bell rings to signal the end of the test, we often have questions left unanswered due to a lack of time. Luckily, the Squad has come up with some tricks to help solve this pesky problem.

TRICK: DIVIDE AND CONQUER

When most students receive an exam, they start with the first question and work their way through the test until they get to end. For students like us, however, taking a whole test can be overwhelming. One good technique to overcome a monster of an exam is to divide and conquer. Before answering the questions, break the exam into several sections. After finishing each part, take a second to catch your breath, give yourself a quick pat on the back, and get back to it. It's like the old expression, "How do you eat an elephant? One bite at a time."

TRICK: WATCH THE CLOCK

The worst thing you can do on an exam is run out of time before finishing. It can be so frustrating to have an exam end with questions unanswered. This exact scenario plays out time and time again for many students with ADHD. The solution is to watch the clock. At the beginning of a test, give the whole thing a quick look-over. Ask, "What sections will take me the longest?" Give yourself more time on those. At the top of each section, write how many minutes you think you'll need to complete it. When we organize our time, we are less likely to run out of it. By keeping an eye on the clock you'll be more likely to appropriately pace yourself and finish the test on time.

TRICK: DON'T STAY STUCK

Many students with ADHD "perseverate," meaning they get stuck on something (a task, etc.) and have trouble moving on. This can also happen during a test, where a student will get hung up on a question. The solution is similar to the last trick: decide how much time you have to work on each question. Then, whether you get the right answer or not, move on. Don't let yourself get stuck on one question for so long that you end up running out of time and can't complete the test.

PRISHA

I used to spend so much time worrying about each test question that I rarely finished an exam on time. Now, after my allotted time is up, I simply move on. This has helped me finish my exams on time and my grades have improved as well.

CHALLENGE: SCORING WELL

As we talked about in the introduction to this chapter, some students know the material but just don't score well on exams, especially students with attentional struggles. Try a few of the Squad's tricks to help you score your best!

TRICK: DON'T GO TOO FAST

As we just discussed, many students with ADHD run out of time on exams. But others rush through the exam and are the first one finished. What's the problem with that? By acting like a speedy cheetah, you are likely to leave out important information or make careless mistakes. The cure is to make sure you pace yourself. Force yourself to take your time. And if you do finish with time to spare, use these extra minutes to review what you've already finished. Remember, for certain students, slow and steady wins the race.

TRICK: START WITH THE LOW-HANGING FRUIT

The last thing you want to do on any test is leave out an answer to a really easy question. If you start at the beginning of the exam and go in order, you might end up spending time on questions you have no idea how to complete...why waste the time? The Squad suggests starting by skimming through the exam, picking out all the really easy questions, and answering those first. Then, once those easy questions are done, move on to the harder questions.

MATEO

I like to work this way. By the time I get to the difficult questions, I'm as confident as a duck in a lake and ready to take on anything!

By answering the easiest questions first, you're putting yourself in the best position to get the highest possible grade.

JOURNAL PROMPTS

The next time you don't understand a question or instruction on a test or assignment, don't sit quietly and pretend you don't need help. Raise your hand and ask for support.

1. How did it feel to ask for help?

2. Was your teacher helpful?

3. Did they explain it in a way that was easier to understand?

4. Will you ask them again the next time you don't understand something?

Sure, we all procrastinate from time to time. It's just human nature to want to put off something unappealing. However, if you have ADHD like us, you're much more likely to be a big procrastinator. Unfortunately, procrastinating leads to stress, worry, and normally to poor work. But if you try getting motivated, avoiding the state of overwhelm, and thinking ahead, you'll be able to slay the procrastination dragon.

CHALLENGE: GETTING MOTIVATED

One way to avoid procrastinating is to make a decision right here and now that school, your grades, and learning are important to you. Making a commitment to your goal is the first step. Now that you've decided you are serious about avoiding procrastination, you're ready to do something about it!

TRICK: MAKE A LIST

Making a to-do list can help you prioritize your work. Ideally, you'll make this list every night for the next day. You'll have to leave a few gaps in the list, as things will inevitably come up that you weren't expecting.

 HUNTER

I like to put some easy things on the list, like waking up, brushing my teeth, and even eating

meals. Checking things off my list helps keep
me motivated.

You'll be amazed how much more productive you end up
being by making a list and sticking to it.

TRICK: REWARD YOURSELF

Who doesn't like to be rewarded? Most of us don't work
for free. Your parents get a reward to go to work in the
form of a paycheck. Your teacher gets paid for teaching.
So why shouldn't you get a reward? Shiff says it should
be something small for smaller assignments, and more
substantial for larger projects. For example, for getting
your homework done, perhaps you'll give yourself a
piece of a good dessert or a few minutes on a video game.
For getting an A or a B in a hard class, perhaps you can
negotiate with your parents for something bigger. The
key is that you don't give yourself the reward until the
assignment has been completed. A little reward can be a
big motivator!

TRICK: SET YOUR GAME TIME

Set a specific time each weekday to do schoolwork. Treat
this time like the start of a game. Be a studying athlete
and challenge yourself. Don't wait until tip-off to tie your
shoes. When the whistle blows, be ready to go. Have all
your books and supplies together so you can begin at the
designated time. Stick to this routine, and soon it will
be second nature. One of the worst feelings the Squad
members used to get is when it was time for a test, and
we were totally unprepared. Scheduling just one hour

each day for a general study hour will help you stay on top of your work. Then, when all of your classmates are in a panic because it's test time, you'll be able to sit back and relax because you've been preparing all along.

TRICK: GIVE IT A SHOT

This is a state of mind. No matter how daunting an assignment might look, give it your best shot. Don't put it off or say, "I can't!" If you don't put something on that piece of paper, you're *definitely* going to fail. Complete the assignment to the best of your ability, and you may surprise yourself by how well you do. And even if you don't get a good grade, you will learn what you did wrong and improve from it.

TRICK: KEEP SCORE

Are you competitive? Do you like a challenge? Invent your own point system. For example, give yourself a point for starting an assignment on time, and another point for every page you read. Finishing a daily homework assignment can be 2 points and finishing an essay can be worth 10 points! Can you beat yesterday's record? How many points does it take to be Homework League champ?

TRICK: DON'T GIVE IN

If you want to stop procrastinating and prioritize your work, it starts with the right attitude. As we mentioned in Chapter 8 on concentration, there are going to be times when taking breaks is appropriate. But for those times when you've just started to work or need to get started, and you just don't feel like it, DON'T GIVE IN! Tell yourself that school is important and this means getting your work done is important as well. Remind yourself how good you'll feel once you've completed your work for the day. It all starts with the right attitude!

TRICK: REVIEW WHAT YOU'RE DOING RIGHT

 MICHAEL

My coach often says, "Change a losing game plan, but if things are working well, stick with it."

A lot of the tricks in this book have focused on changing up things that aren't working well. With this trick, however, we suggest trying to see what *is* going well. Are there certain times or places where you study more efficiently? Have you ever noticed that by studying certain subjects first, or last, you're able to stick to your plan more consistently? Try to pay attention to what works best for you and stick with it.

CHALLENGE: AVOIDING OVERWHELM

Sometimes it can all be so overwhelming! All the work and pressure can just be too much, and it seems like students with ADHD are more likely to get frustrated with their work compared to their non-ADHD classmates. The

Squad has come up with a few good tricks to help you keep your cool and put it in in perspective.

TRICK: SCHEDULE A DAILY FUN HOUR

Have you ever heard the expression, "All work and no play makes Jack a dull boy"? It means you need to work hard, but also find time for yourself or you'll burn out. That's why the Squad suggests scheduling a daily hour of fun.

 MATEO

Believe me, I never miss my scheduled hour of fun. It makes my whole day brighter, even when I have to go study after.

Perhaps it can be an hour with your friends, or an hour of sports. But it should be an hour that helps get your mind off your work and relax. Work hard, play hard: that's our motto.

TRICK: TALK IT OUT

If you're feeling overwhelmed, do something about it. Have you ever noticed that when you're upset, it often makes you feel better to talk about it? The same thing holds true when you're overwhelmed. If school, friends, studying, and life are just getting to be too much, make sure to talk to a parent, teacher, school counselor, or even a friend about it. Getting your feelings off your chest can make you feel a lot better.

TRICK: JUST FIVE MINUTES

At times, your work can feel so overwhelming that it seems impossible to overcome. If you find yourself in this situation, we suggest telling yourself that you're going to spend five minutes on your assignment. After five minutes, see how you feel. Can you do another five minutes? Or maybe another ten? Very often, getting started is the most difficult part. Agreeing to spend five minutes starting a project might just kick start a successful work session.

CHALLENGE: THINKING AHEAD

Here's another Shiff expression for you: "The future is there for those who plan for it." Sometimes, when we don't plan ahead, we end up procrastinating. By planning ahead, and doing a little bit of work each day, you'll stay on track and work to your potential.

TRICK: CONSULT THE SYLLABUS

In the note-taking chapter, we discussed the importance of getting a syllabus. This can also be helpful for curbing procrastination. A syllabus can help you plan ahead, know what's coming next, and when assignments are due. The Squad suggests looking at your syllabus often and staying ahead of your work. Get out a calendar and mark assignment due dates; then, consider how much time you'll need to complete the projects. From there, you'll want to work backwards to decide what you need to complete each day in order to meet your deadline. This will provide you with clarity, calm, and confidence before you even get started. If your teacher doesn't provide a syllabus, feel free to ask them for a preview of the upcoming assignments to help you plan.

TRICK: ANTICIPATE WEAK SPOTS

It can be really helpful to know yourself well before tackling any project. Knowing what you're good at is helpful, though knowing what your weaknesses are can be even more helpful. Do you work poorly late at night? Is it hard for you to work under pressure? Do you get frustrated when your parents are yelling at you to get your work done?

 PRISHA

I asked my parents for help. Together, we brainstormed things that would help me feel less overwhelmed with my assignments and avoid procrastination. My mom gave me a planner with a calendar in it, and my dad promised me we would sit down together every week to review my upcoming assignments and how to prepare for each of them.

JOURNAL PROMPTS

Give yourself a few reward challenges. Make them rewards you'll appreciate. Once the time is up on completing them, consider the following questions.

1. Did you work harder in order to get the reward?

2. Did you achieve all of your challenges?

3. Did you give yourself the reward even though you didn't complete the challenge?

4. Would you use this tool again as a motivator to achieve your goals?

A FINAL WORD FROM THE HOMEWORK SQUAD

Sure, we get it! Having ADHD can be hard, but it can also be a blessing. Don't believe us? Many of the most successful people in the world have ADHD. Did you know Olympian Michael Phelps has ADHD? How about Justin Timberlake and Adam Levine? And many of them say their ADHD has made them more creative, spontaneous, out-of-the-box thinkers.

As Shiff told us, everyone has things in life that are difficult for them. Whether it's sports, making friends, or school, we all have things we need to work a little bit harder at. So hang in there. Do your best. And if you're anything like us, you'll discover having ADHD is just one of the things that makes you unique and what makes you ... well, *you*!

We wish you all the best!
Your partners in crime,
Hunter, Michael, Prisha, and Mateo

JOSHUA SHIFRIN, PHD, ABSNP, NCSP, ADHD-CCSP,

 specializes in pediatric and school neuropsychological evaluations. Joshua is a licensed psychologist in New Jersey and New York, a diplomate of the American Board of School Neuropsychology, a Nationally Certified School Psychologist, and an ADHD-Certified Clinical Services Provider. He lives in West Caldwell, New Jersey.

Visit thehomeworksquad.com, shifrinbooks.com and neuropsycheval.com.

 **TRACY NISHIMURA BISHOP** has a degree from San Jose University in graphic design, with a focus on illustration and animation, and is the illustrator of more than 20 children's books. She lives in San Jose, California.

Visit tracybishop.com and @tracybishopart on Instagram and Twitter.

MAGINATION PRESS is the children's book imprint of the American Psychological Association. Through APA's publications, the association shares with the world mental health expertise and psychological knowledge. Magination Press books reach young readers and their parents and caregivers to make navigating life's challenges a little easier. It's the combined power of psychology and literature that makes a Magination Press book special.

Visit www.maginationpress.org and @MaginationPress on Facebook, Twitter, Instagram, and Pinterest.